Breathing Aether: A Collection Of Poems

By Jarod Tanzer

Copyright © 2019 by Jarod Tanzer.
All rights reserved.

Published by Jarod Tanzer,
Margaretville, NY

No part of this publication may be reproduced, distributed, or transmitted in any form or by any means, including photocopying, recording, or other electronic or mechanical methods, without the prior written permission of the publisher, except in the case of brief quotations embodied in critical reviews and certain other noncommercial uses permitted by copyright law.

Any resemblance to actual persons, living or dead, events, or locales is entirely coincidental.

ISBN: 978-0-578-59699-0

Book and cover design by Jarod Tanzer

For permission to reprint portions of this book, or to order a review copy, contact:
jmtanzer@hotmail.com

To All My Friends and Family

ACKNOWLEDGMENTS

This chapbook wouldn't have come into being without the help of Meagan Downing; copyeditor and dear friend. I couldn't have gone on this journey without you. Here's to many more.

Invisible are the bonds between us.
Breathe, and they are revealed.

AN EXERCISE IN BREAKING WRITER'S BLOCK

Start
With anything
Words
That happen to fall
From head space
No net
To catch
No screen
To sift
Forget the filter
Let syllables fall
As they may
Make a mess
Into a masterpiece
Mad cap mosaics
Capturing captions
To explain
A brainstorm
Disregard form
Until
It transforms
On its own accord
Syntax in discord
According to the code
Of chaos
Order comes
At the end.

WHIRL'D

Surrounded
By circles
Cyclical patterns
Of repeating rigmarole
Long lasting loops
Of everlasting infinities
Twirling
Into one another
Crashing and fusing
Like unruly, winding rivers
Intertwining energies
Symbiotic synergies
Swirling
Twisting in space-time
I'll converge with yours
If you collide with mine.

STRANDED

There really is no way
To certainty
Other than waiting
Wading
Within this river *temporalis*
Sluggish here
Swiftly sweeping there
There must be another way
Maybe even over
These wanton waters
I just want to look
A glimpse
At what I wonder about
So I wander about
Wishing to discover a path
A place
A shortcut over time-space
A free ride
From the boundaries of now
To the banks of what will be.

SPONTANEOUS HUMAN CONNECTION

Spontaneously
Worlds once separate…now meet
A simple greeting.

HERE AND NOW, THERE AND THEN

Many lifetimes passed
Seen and felt
With inherited breath
Forgotten it all
But in flashes
Flickers of memory
Reacquainted, reunited
With everyone you once were.

BRAIN STORMED

Experiencing torrential storms
In his mind
O, to be a cloud
Caught in that mental typhoon!
One would surely
Be in for quite a ride...
And O,
To be the sun
In this restless psyche!
Such glory one would claim
In taming
Such a terrific tempest!

NITROVASCULARGLYCERIN

Pumping hard
Shakes his soul
Thumping louder
Throws his thoughts off course
Burning blood
Chars the chambers of his chest
Scorching the sanctums of his psyche
Desire fire
Roaring strong
For as long as he can remember
Combusting so carelessly
It's far too easy
To fall far too fast.

WAITING FOR TWILIGHT

Looking up
All he sees is
This vast sheet of sapphire
Covering his beloved stars
The yellow king dominates the sky
Not even casual clouds
Dare to enter its domain
Yet he defies its radiant rule
Fighting the far away inferno
With heartfelt fire
A small sun in his soul
Fueled
By inhaling airborne auroras
Because when this day of naked sky
Dims down
A beguiling night will follow
Dressed
In her sparkling gown.

ACROSS A CROWDED ROOM

I am taken by the wake
Of words we don't share
Drowning
In this ocean of noise
The wave of silence between us
The sea is too wild
No way to navigate
To your glance
Look at me and smile
Once more
Something to swim toward
Lighthouse of your soul
Your lips
A beacon in dark din
I can't hear words
Though
I can tell the direction
Out of nowhere
Out of the blue
Like the deep indigo
I willingly jumped into
Because
My ship was swiftly sailing
Drifting
Somewhere else
My one chance
To reach shore
And hear your words
No longer drowned out
By crashing conversation.

NOWHERE TO EXPLODE

Attempting to contain a star
Reeling in the blast
Each time it erupts
An astronomic challenge
Have you ever tried to hold captive
A hypernova?

It burns every time
Sinew splitting shotgun blasts
From inside your sternum
Ribs
Can only cage such high gauge combustion
For just so long
Can only withstand so much
Before it's wracked
Wrecked from within

You can't even begin to comprehend
The strength required
To stomach such an internal onslaught
From one's own organs
With the feeling that
If you stop
Dangerous pain might catch up
And you'll drop from the damage

When blood
From the freshly ripped stitches of your heart
Finally floods your brain
The overworked electric impulses
Jolt the big boss blood chamber

Into a false sense of elation
Impatient
It beats
Until it blows

So
Feel
If you dare
But be prepared to defend
Against impending inner impact
And to react to any aftershock
That may rock your body
In a relapse
See if you can resist collapse
Because that's what happens
When that star inside
Has nowhere to explode.

IT'S ALL IN MY HEAD

I can't explain
Why my brain remains strained
By constant cognitive chaos
Deus ex Machina
The tick tock
This mental metronome
Rocks me like clockwork
And I just can't stop it
From jerking me around

I know
It sounds like my wits are unwound
But I'm grounded
I swear
My mind is too heavy
To stay up in the air
Repairs
Will be have to rationed
As rationality is ravaged
And reason is ripped apart
Seems like I'm beginning to be finished
I just don't know where to start

The walls
Give way to the corrosion
And contents of my brain burst out
Expect an explosion
Colors and scenes
Of visions and dreams
Gush and rush
Their luster

It gleams!

Finally
See what storms inside me
Daily
From the moment I wake
To the extent of my REM state
This biological mechanism
Is merely a vessel
For ethereal expression
As a result of that concussion
I no longer possess the ability
To exercise discretion
I'm afraid
All I can offer is this confession:
It's all in my head.

LONGING FOR LINGUISTICS

I would like
To be able
To speak
Every language.
To listen
And have the chance
To relate
Despite
Vibrational barriers.
To extend
Connection
Beyond
Familiar phonetics.
To have
A clearer view
Of human similarities
No longer shrouded
In
Wayward words.
Not one nuance
Not a single inflection
Lost
In translation.

ASTRAL PLANE AND SIMPLE

From the deepest reaches of oblivion
To the heights of far too much
We can take the scenic route
Through everything between.

CRIME OF PASSION

If I could sneak into the space
Behind your lovely face
Like a thief of thoughts
I'd case the place
Smell the flowers of how you really feel
Then steal the vase
I'd be quite satisfied
With that little memento of your mind
Though you've got lots of pretty dreams in there
That's all I came to find
So with a wave of my cape
I'd make my escape
And leave my calling card behind.

SEASONAL STIMULI

Seeing
With the sun's shining resolution
Listening
Through the leaves in flowing frequencies
Speaking
With the snow's soft and subtle voice
Feeling
The surrounding world
With flower flooded fingers
Senses
Sewn to seasons.

BLUE-GRAY SERENADE

What was blue
Has now turned gray
The sky's mood has swayed
A graceful turn for the worse
Her azure shine slips
Into a silver shade of melancholy
She weeps, spills her life to me
Brandishing her anger
She strikes the earth
My heart
She sleeps, whispers secrets in the night
In the wake of her tempestuous tirade
I awaken, miss the thunder
She slumbers late
Only to rise
And shine sapphires
As I await
Another storm.

LIGHT YEAR LIMITS

I stand inside the Universe
Tall against its torrent
And never fail to falter
I lay conquered, give a smile
My vengeful eyes shoot upward
A visceral vow of victory
I retreat to the sanctuary of my psyche
And tend to my wounds
Sounds of inner tunes resonate through reason
My muse is motivation
With meditation as my wind
I'll soon sail beyond the stars
And stand outside.

LORD OF THE LITTLE

On a throne of dirt, he reigns
Until the rain washes away his empire

He rebuilds on mud
A glorious, sinking kingdom
This puddle is his moat
Until the sun dries up his defenses

Dead weed fences
Hold his insect enemies at bay
Until the wasps swarm from above

His pebble cannons fire
Thwarting the airborne assailants
Wailing trumpets herald his triumph
Until an army of giants trample his domain

Conquered he remains
Until he rebuilds on rocks

Stocks up on resilience
Come water, war, fire, or disaster
Chaos will call him master

He shall retain small world sovereignty
His majesty, King
Of the ant hill.

SKY CHILDREN

We were pulled together
By the gravity of our destiny
Despite being weighed down
By our questions of the past

Under the shroud of sinister clouds
On that darkest of days
We found each other
This world had never seen such a blaze

It was the brightest of nights
And even as we burned
Hearts splitting in nuclear fission
We smiled

We discovered
What makes us glow.

LOVE TRIANGLE

O, Mistress Sky
And Madame Earth
I love you both so much

One so far
You leave me dreaming

One so close
We touch

You, so high
Enchant my eyes
I try to climb the air
And when I fall back down
With open ground
You hold me as I lie there

I'd surely die without you, Sky
My breath would go astray
I cannot live without you, Earth
I'd surely drift away

So Sky,
I'll just keep chasing you
Continue gazing into space

And Earth,
I'll never leave you
Your lovely face holds me in place.

$ICK

Avast ye knave!
Slave to corpulent corruption!
You couldn't make a change
With four quarters
And that's at a novice level
Revel, you will
Still in stagnant avarice
Hurry now
Howl at that monetary moon
You foul buffoon
Your balloon is bound to burst
Doom will quench your gluttonous thirst
Now and forever
Your malevolent endeavor
Is guided by green devils
Their lips drip with acidic saliva
Survivor will not be your moniker
My demonic sir,
You cannot take it with you.

LADY IN THE SKY

Dressed in blue
She beckons
I cannot turn away

Dressed in red
She ravages
I cannot disobey

Dressed in white
She whispers
With my senses she does play

Dressed in black
She keeps me waiting
Staring at the sky for days.

MEOW

You are cloaked in mystery
Draped in capes so dark
All I can see are those eyes
Like a witchcraft cat
You slip through the cracks
And I'm the dog that chases your glances
I'm taking my chances
Stumbling through shadows
You evade my advances
Those eyes
Wild
Like a spellbound cat
They're all I can see in this world dyed black
I can't help but smile
Those eyes have me mesmerized
With that feline style.

CANVAS

She says sunshine hurts her eyes
And the raindrops make her cold
Doesn't see the shine in gold
And silver stings her soul
If only I could dip a bush
Into night sky or the snow
Paint some light into her heart with white
And see her glow in indigo.

A SENSE OF ZEN

Hearing a leaf
Hitting the surface of a pond
And the ripples that follow
The sound silence makes
Beyond the song of nature

Watching a flower petal
Gliding downstream
And how slowly it goes
The moment you see it
In the rush of a waterfall

It is presence
And absence

Nothing
Everything.

DESPERADO

Yeah, you're some kind of beautiful
Now you really got me stunned
Just a single glance, a sucker punch
From a hundred hefty guns

Easy with those eyes now, girl
A fella could get hurt
Well, it's a lovely way to end my days
Give me one last gaze and leave my body in the dirt

Careful with that heart there, cowgirl
See, I've lost some duels before
And I'm in your line of fire now...

Wish I was who you're aiming for.

DANGEROUS GAME

You say
I shouldn't even think of you
That you'll hurt me so bad
Like playing Russian roulette
For bragging rights,
You're not worth the risk
But to forget you;
I'd have to lose that match
Point blank gun blast
And I'd still survive
Still alive after round one
To get the job done
It would at least take two
Then the moment my eyes closed
I'd be dreaming of you

You say
I should just give up on you
That you'll really mess me up
Like playing William Tell
For the hell of it,
I'm crazy for staring down that arrow
But to throw away hope;
Now that would tear me apart
Ten million spears
Driven directly through my heart
So I'll stand and take my chances
With your brand of pain
Rain your arrows on me, let them fall
On my nonexistent stronghold
I'll take it all with open chest

And still refuse the blindfold

You say
I'd be better off without you
That I should run and save myself
Like playing hop-scotch
At hyper speed
I'd be a fool to stay at square one
But turning away;
It's impossible, you see?
You've grasped me tightly with your gravity
I'm falling in your atmosphere
Despite the fear,
I want to dive into your sky
You say
I'll be incinerated
But I'll risk it
Every time.

CANDY

A simple wink
And you have me hooked
With addictive conviction
Adept at enchantment
You know those eyes are dangerous
Yet you flaunt them
Without regard
Killing me in cold blood
It complements the temperature of sweat
That emerges
Amidst such fleeting heat
Burning my bravery
Freezing my fortitude
I abandon all logic
For that piece of passing passion
Ephemeral euphoria
That taste
Of sugar-coated cruelty
Sweet bitterness remains
And you are long gone
I walk with my withdrawals
Praying I bump into a fix.

SNOW SOUNDS

What would you call it?
The sound snow makes
Under your boots
A creak?
Or a crunch?
A downtrodden moan
From underfoot oppression
I believe I've found
The one nameless sound
In existing English
The only orphan onomatopoeia
The shriek of crystals crushed
Killed
By a stroll
The noise is truly chilling
Every step
A violent vibration
Pleasant to the ears
Each crunch
Every creak
I'd call it a *creach*!
For lack of a better word.

FINDING TIME

Take me back to the days
When life was a mystery
To the beginning of my history
When the sun stayed strong
When procrastinating nightfall
Came along slow
When I did not search so frantically
For clues
The road is littered
With crooked lines and landmines
So my time cord unwinds
And I pick up the slack
Reading every fiber
I left back among footsteps
Ones that reflect echoes
Of younger days

SAY NO TO A SLOW DAY

My body soaks up the boredom
And my brain follows suit
The fruits of creation
Have long since rotted
Seeds eaten
By predatory passersby
Why the tormenting lack of passion plagues me
I'll never know
No longer can I grow
In the absence of nomadic nutrition
My position is glued
Roots clinging
Deep into sofa cushions
Adhered to screens
Dreams are mere memories
Vaguely recalled
I collect fragments of stimuli
With self-induced serenity
My affinity for inkblot lyrics
Long since cured
As absurd as it sounds
I'm astounded by self-contempt
So I attempt to ignite my head
As I'm a perfect match
For the written word
With my vision no longer blurred
The blank page burns my eyes
Pen flies deftly
A rapier
In D'artagnan's hand
Infused

With motion from the muses
They must like me
Now you can call me Nike
Because my middle name is Victory
Triumphant
Over television trickery
Inspired
No longer hard-wired to the glitch
Scratched my itchy imagination
Detached from the trap
Of everyday complacency.

COMBAT CONCERTO

Hail to the guns that fire for a living
    To the bullets that do the work
Hail to hands
      Constricting triggers with conviction
And to soldiers
      So sKILLfully berserk

The madness is magnificent!
    To rapid fire rhythm
The enemy will sing
     Oh, the horror of the harmony
In sanguine symphonies
      It rings

Supersonic s t a c c a t o plays
    Bass drums break the heavens
Five star conductors
      Raise their batons
  A violent dance begins.

OF LIFE AND BUBBLES

In an act
Of sheer desperation
Bubbles rise
Rapidly
In a futile attempt
To escape
A violent, inevitable
Fate
Sudden, unpredictable
Explosion
On our plane of consciousness
They merely
Vanish
Blink
Out of existence
Rainbow swirled spheres
Transparent
Delicate
So fragile
Are we the same?

TWO

Two souls
Playing tag
One is quicker
Younger
But the other
Knows the game
It's always
A tie.

LISTEN

She asked me

What it was like

What it meant

To let go

I told her

She'd find the answer

In the things

She whispered to me.

RETROSPECTACLES

I wonder
What nothing looks like
The closest image
I can visualize
Is endless black
Or white
But see,
Even black and white
Are something
A singularity
Glares at me
But I don't know where to look
20/20
Just isn't enough
If only I was a special type
Of farsighted
A reverse clairvoyant
I could spy
With my little eye
A big bang
Find the frame of mind
To rewind time
Before the blast
Just before Genesis
So I would know
For future reference.

THE SOUND OF EVERYTHING

The sound of everything
Rarely
Rings all at once
Typically
It comes in fragments
As we pass through existence
Alarms, yawns
Cracking joints
Rushing faucets
Falling to drips
Dishes clacking
Drawers swooshing
Locks clicking
Keys jingling
Engines crescendo
And decrescendo
Driving horn sections
Brakes squealing
Elevators ding
Fluorescent lights hum
Clocks ticking
And tocking
Sound by sound
As we muddle
And meander through
But
Every now and then
Someone stops
Listens
As the sound of everything
Rings all at once.

UNCENSORED SENSORY

We could feel the earth breathe
It flooded, a great wind
Combining
Our lungs with the leaves
We could see veins in the sky
They stretched, vast branches
Connecting
To the ones in our eyes
We could hear music from space
It flowed, stellar symphonies
Composing
Crescendos from the commonplace
We could smell so much stardust
It spilled, swirling clouds
Colliding
Our vows and our lust
We could taste each other's heartbeat
They echoed, drums of thunder
Confessing
Truth
Abstract, concrete
Never ending, complete.

www.ingramcontent.com/pod-product-compliance
Lightning Source LLC
Chambersburg PA
CBHW021001090426
42736CB00010B/1411